Mark Cole

FOUR
TEXAS
QUARTETS

Thank you to my family and T.S. Eliot

Mark Cole
www.bymarkcole.com

For all Texans, everywhere

Especially for those not here yet

INTRODUCTION

What follows is a loose rendering of T.S. Eliot's final poetic output, *Four Quartets*, but for and about Texas and Texans. In places, I try to mimic *Four Quartets* very precisely, in other places more loosely, and in others not at all. Hopefully the work in its entirety will accomplish at least two things.

First, I hope it will direct my fellow Texans (and Texans to be) to Eliot, the real Poet, the source of wisdom and poetic insight and inspiration. If you engage with Eliot's entire poetic output, and I hope you do, the intellectual, emotional and spiritual payoff might well be immense and life changing.

Second, I hope to harness a little bit of Eliot's technique of loose correspondence to existing poetic forms; concrete images and sensory engagement; the duplicity and richness of words; allusions to history, literature and myth, abrupt and rapid movement between and among people, places and time; question and answer and other nearly imperceptible patterns; intermittent philosophical discourse and internal dramatic monologue, and all of this to slowly delineate a theme which continually gathers weight and majesty until it is complete (but never done). And the theme in *Four Texas Quartets* is Texas, and what Texas means, which is freedom.

Eliot wrote within the context of the entire western intellectual, literary and spiritual tradition. Dante stands out as particularly important to Eliot. Dante's task and his accomplishment is comprehensive: he gives us a visionary and metaphysical *summum bonum*, an ascending journey which is completed with a glimpse of the Love that moves the sun and the stars, the Triune God. Eliot wisely defers to Dante, and so his *summum bonum*, though a reconciliation of past present and future and thus of eternity, remains within the realm of creation. Eliot does set forth Christ's promise to us, and in doing that, he shows us a way to cope with being human. But the subject matter for Eliot is ultimately humanity; yes, humanity's relationship to eternity, but nonetheless Eliot quite consciously does not ascend to the heights of Dante's beatific vision and apprehension of the Trinity.

The subject matter of *Four Texas Quartets* is closer still to the ground, humanity in its terrestrial workings, the coming and going of civilization; conflict, borders, language, change; family, creation, work and hardship, and thus the nature of freedom. And *Four Texas Quartets* is about a finite (though vast) and particular location which, like most places, is simply a microcosm of the human story. The story of Texas is understood best as the story of freedom and its unfolding, its ebbing and flowing; its gains and losses, its continual development and decay and rebirth.

Texas and T.S. Eliot may not be an obvious fit. But bringing Texas and Eliot together, given my life, seems unavoidable. Eliot has accompanied me for about a fourth of my life so far, and I will not be putting him down. He gave me a way to make sense out of the carnage that was the 20th century, and a way to cope with what may well be nightmarish in the 21st. He showed me how to love equally tradition and innovation. He has given me immense personal comfort during life's difficulties, including the death of family members. I've seen him do the same for others. I've had the privilege of introducing him and reading him alongside others. To say I'm grateful for the life and work of Thomas Sterns Eliot sounds glib, but other than quoting his own poetry back to him, I'm not sure what else can be said. He was of course acutely aware of the limits of words and language, so I feel somewhat in good company by not knowing what to say other than thank you, to him and to our Lord whom he faithfully served.

Eliot also compelled me, over time, to plunge more deeply into Texas, and likewise, I will not be putting this down. This is where my life-thought has brought me. Eliot famously said that most people should never leave their hometown. I understand this now, and for the most part, agree entirely. He also acknowledged that some were to leave and go elsewhere and this is of course the journey he took. When *Four Quartets* was published, he had been a citizen of the United Kingdom for some time and a figure of global renown, having moved far from his native St. Louis. He also sets forth a third possibility: that some can travel and explore and read and study, but then use all of that in furtherance of civilization in their homes. As he says near the end of *Little Girding*:

We shall not cease from exploration
And the end of all our exploring
Will be to arrive where we started
And know the place for the first time.

This is the path that I am on. I was born in Oklahoma, but moved to Farwell, in the Texas Panhandle, in the third grade; my wife was born in England, but grew up in Dublin. My children are all native Texans, but have lived and traveled extensively outside of Texas, mostly in green, temperate, mosquito-, snake- and hurricane-free Ireland. I lived in Waco as a college student, and moved with Shona, my Irish wife, to Houston to practice law. Our family has mostly grown up in Montgomery County, established in 1837 by the Republic of Texas. Uniquely situated, Montgomery County seems to be the beginning of the Piney Woods of East Texas, but without fully leaving behind the Texas Gulf Coast. I've had the privilege of serving in local government in Montgomery County. The people here are honest, hard-working, generous, patriotic, freedom-loving and God-fearing. In short, they are Texans. We are blessed to live among them. We hope to travel and even live part-time in other parts of Texas, but Montgomery County is our home.

My intellectual journey has meandered through English literature (mostly prose) and political philosophy as an undergrad, followed by German language study and graduate school in philosophy, theology and law in New England, Germany, Liechtenstein, Dublin, the Midwest and London. After becoming a lawyer, I put the horse back in front of the cart, and seriously studied the Bible and then over time found poetry becoming increasingly important to me, with philosophy diminishing in importance. And then somewhere in there I discovered Eliot, both his poetry and his prose. My dissertation in the history of ideas has one chapter expressly devoted to Eliot, but in truth, it is an extended application of his thought to the history of the culture of the west. And once that was done, other writers like John Graves, Wendell Berry, J. Frank Dobie, and Larry McMurtry began to speak to me.

In continually returning to Texas for the first time, I have grown obsessed with our land, our history, our food, our music, our traditions, our people and our industries. Texas has been good to me and my family. I hope to treat it with the honor and respect and love that it deserves. If nothing else, *Four Texas Quartets* is my first love letter to Texas.

Hopefully there are unfamiliar words and names in what follows, and I am hopeful that you will do some additional reading and research and dig in to these Texas names, places, people and their stories. You will be rewarded. Our history is rich.

In fact, our history is prohibitively vast, intricate and abundant, if one wants to write about Texas. Only a few of the major traditions and strands of Texanness are explored here with even partial adequacy. With time and space, I would love every cultural-ethnic-linguistic tradition and heritage to be explored equally. But with constraints (and constraints are good), *Four Texas Quartets* only touches upon a few. In *Lincolnville*, the compound ghost figure (borrowed directly from Eliot, as his readers will immediately recognize) is composed of three great but very different Texans: Davy Crockett, Lightnin' Hopkins and Elisabet Ney.

Crockett represents the tradition of Texans who rushed in from other parts of the United States, for various reasons, but related ultimately to opportunity, pioneering, a fresh start, a challenge, in short, for freedom. He also represents the countless Texas pioneers – most of whom were not famous at all – who died violently in their freedom quest and were never properly buried.

Lightnin' Hopkins represents those descendants of slaves who once freed became pioneering farmers, then gravitated to cities (and in his case, to Houston) in search of opportunity and modern convenience. Lightnin' is also a first tier figure in Texas music, a Godfather of Texas blues, and therefore all Texas music in its vast intricate musical fabric comprised of Western Swing, country, blues, jazz; spirituals, gospel, rock, Tex-Mex, Cajun and the folk and classical music of Czech, German and other European immigrants.

Elisabet Ney represents the mid-19th century humanistic and Utopian European immigrant pioneers who believed in communities founded upon high ideals, often socialist and free thinking. Over the years Texas projects included health and work utopias, as well as Quaker, Catholic and other Christian experiments. Elisabet Ney also represents the many great Texans who brought high culture and fine art to the dangerous Texas wilderness, and did so pretty early in our history. She and countless others like her are major civilizing forces. Though Texas is a place of rough and tumble, agriculture, manual labor and extreme weather, it is also a place which has never lacked for high culture because of people like Elisabet Ney. I'm so grateful for them.

The tradition which I personally identify with most closely, namely, non-utopian, American Protestant (and more precisely, Baptist) Christian missionary pioneers, educators, lawyers and builders of civilization, I feel like are given short shrift in *Four Texas Quartets*, though the frequent references to Baylor University and thus its Baptist pioneer founders, perhaps will make up for that. Also given short shrift is the Mexican (and reaching further back, Spanish) influence which constitutes so much of Texas. Then there is our Native American history. And East Texas. Volumes could also be written about Germans and Czechs in Texas, not to mention Moravians, Hungarians, Slovaks and Poles. Much more needs to be said about Texas and Texans and the Civil War.

When I consider all that, *Four Texas Quartets* seems ridiculously inadequate. No omissions in *Four Texas Quartets* should be interpreted as disrespect or lack of interest or awareness; I am in awe of each of these strands of history and tradition, but the poem that follows is meant to be representative and suggestive, not comprehensive, so choices and therefore omissions must be made. I am comforted by the fact that Eliot does not give us a comprehensive didactic account of European Christian civilization, and does not recount all of the Biblical promises Christ made in detail. So it is here. *Four Texas Quartets* is partial, and a first effort. I hope to right omissions in future writing.

All human history, including Texas history, is bottomless, elusive, exciting and mysterious yet familiar. But what ties all Texans together is freedom. Freedom is precarious; and it seems, in early 2021, to be more so now than ever. With the Orwellian capabilities of technology now so pervasive, it seems that human civilization is at a crossroads and freedom seems to be undervalued. The quest for safety seems to be the universal priority. Moreover, there are no wildernesses where freedom loving pioneers can go. There's not another Texas to go settle; we have to make do with the one we have, for freedom's sake.

I do believe – completely – that it was for freedom that Texas was birthed. That's what the greatest Texan, Sam Houston, believed also. And Texas has always been a place where freedom-lovers go and are welcomed. I do not know precisely what actions should be taken at this time, or really any other time, in order to preserve and extend human freedom. But I do know that if the value of freedom burns deeply in our chests, then the details as to how freedom is to be preserved and enhanced for ourselves and posterity will take care of themselves through the actions of freedom-loving people, in time. But if the desire for freedom fades, then freedom will be lost until it wakes again. My hope is that *Four Texas Quartets* will fan the flame of freedom and perhaps even spark a few brush fires of freedom, in Texas and elsewhere.

FOUR TEXAS QUARTETS

We view ourselves on the eve of battle. We are nerved for the contest, and must conquer or perish. It is vain to look for present aid: none is at hand. We must now act or abandon all hope! Rally to the standard, and be no longer the scoff of mercenary tongues! Be men, be free men, that your children may bless their father's name.

General Sam Houston, *Speech before San Jacinto*

STEAMBOAT HOUSE

The earth is mostly just a boneyard. But pretty in the sunlight.

Larry McMurtry, Lonesome Dove

Houston, Tranquility Base here. The Eagle has landed.

Neil Armstrong, July 20, 1969

῝Ως οἵ γ' ἀμφίεπον τάφον ῝Εκτορος ἱπποδάμοιο.

Iliad, Book 24, line 944

Texas will again lift its head and stand among the nations. It ought to do so, for no country upon the globe can compare with it in natural advantages.

Sam Houston

I

Yesterday melts into today

But today bleeds into tomorrow

Before we know it's here

And the future is nothing anyways

Except the past vaulting forward

Memories now masquerade

As future predicted projected and anticipated.

But yet it's undeniable: whatever time is

We are in it.

Stories told songs sung events remembered

Only in time

Tales exaggerated perceptions intensified friends eulogized

Only in time

Grudges nursed losses elegized forgiveness proffered

Only in time

Memories harden now is lived and next year imagined

Only in time.

Where does the wind begin

And where does it end?

We can imagine what might have been

But it's an illusion

Because what might have been and what has been

Were always one and the same

Not because choices don't matter

But because eternity is now

Beginnings and ends are one and the same

And in this recognition

We are free.

Boots crunch across gravel

A rooster incessantly calls

Enveloped in heat we follow it

Ascend fifteen steep steps

And peer through an undersized window

Into the rented upstairs parlor

That could hold maybe twenty mourners.

Here

The ousted Governor's modest funeral was held

Two years before the mighty scourge of war would pass.

A decent sized home for a normal man

Steamboat House with its wraparound wooden porch

Ridiculed and unwanted by the original owner

Became the Governor's discarded and second hand

Reservation in exile.

Houston's final destination should have been

A mighty fortress of pink granite white limestone and live oak

Heroically rising out of the Texas prairie

Defying hurricanes withstanding heat

A permanent Texas Stonehenge

Nebuchadnezar's Palace

A Parthenon.

But he was eulogized *here* and

Laid to rest by Masonic pallbearers

Who walked silently down muddy roads

Through a steady summer rain

To Oakwood Cemetery where they had misspelled

"Governor" for the

Tennessee period on his monument

Two blocks away a Subway and helpful signs lead us there

On one hand this seems not exactly right

On the other, maybe it is perfect

Because it is Texas.

After Houston died

It took some time

But we put him back in the narrative

During the Depression, we relocated

A restored Steamboat House to this place.

The first spoken word

On the surface of the moon was his name.

His massive likeness keeps watch

Over the road connecting Galveston to Dallas

Today his countenance seems secure

And his presence looms large.

But we also know that storm and frenzy and madness

Can be unfurled

Like an extinct volcano coming to life

Intoxicating emotional spectacle

A veritable witches' sabbath

A shrill whistle of a storm god in a nocturnal forest

And then memory becomes distorted targeted and
destroyed

By tens of thousands emoting screeching and looting

While tens of millions watch the

Psychotic destruction stupefied and paralyzed.

In the shorter term so long as the madness persists

Guillotines may bring statues down

Memory may become corrupted and useless hatreds stoked

But in the longer arc of history

Violent passions will die in fruitless exhaustion

And despair of the waste wrought

The electrifying fury will dissipate

Because lightning cannot compete with the

Vast

Slow-moving

Texas sky

And soon enough like a near-sighted Irish scribbler

Descending from his fortified monastery

Illuminated manuscripts in hand

Our bards will once again

Ploddingly wander the dangerous countryside

And tell the story

Of Houston

Texas

And freedom.

And *in time*

We will put up

That seventy-foot toppled statue of the General

Again.

II

The sea wrought and was tempestuous against them

Like those who cast forth Jonah into the sea

German princes dumped their encumbering patrician titles

Overboard into the briny bubbling drink

And the sea ceased its rage.

Soon they would unaristocratically disembark

Turn their backs to the sea

Forget Europe and begin the long walk

Into a vast dangerous and remote expanse

Without the absurd assertion of noble privilege

Against heat snake tornado and marauder.

Some survived

And of those

A few flourished and savored

The abundance of the earth

Its fruit and fuel

Rapid and new wealth followed

And so was spread a thin civilizing layer of themselves

Over the Texas topsoil

Melding people and place.

Having defeated death and decay for a season

Unable to forget their recent uncertain and violent past

Knowing they will contend tomorrow

With a doubtful inglorious and maybe deadly future

Our ancestors asserted *life*

And thus began

Our fascination with the biggest barns

The craziest landmarks

The hottest peppers

The loudest trucks

And rhinestones:

Celebrate build and spend bigly *now*

Because a freezing Arctic front

Can race from Canada to Texas

In two days

Wreak havoc for three

Then be followed by a rapid thaw

That's a thing and we have a name for it: a blue norther.

We have seen big fortunes quickly won

Spectacularly lost

And so the time is always now

The size always large.

Our pioneering grandparents didn't plant

Churches which grow to more than 10,000 members

But their descendants do

They didn't fry up the Round Rock Donut or trot out Big Bertha

Or build Kyle Field

But we do

We are magnetically genetically and historically drawn to the

Colossal oversized over the top ostentatious assertive and

Just *plain old big.*

Builders of Gothic cathedrals and Texas Stadium

Grasped that size and scale induce awe

Heighten experience

Revive and elevate the soul

To union with God

A call to worship

Or at least to gawk and say *wow.*

Our capitol building and founding obelisk are

Both taller than their counterparts in Washington DC.

But our quest for size also flows from the recognition

That you are real and relevant

And what you do unconstrained

Not pinned in

Actually matters.

Our hardscrabble logic dictates that if pounding a fence post

Into the dirt matters a little

Then pounding a thousand surely matters a lot.

Normal life thus takes on unmysterious meaning and dignity

Merely ornamental gestures from the old world

Were here forgotten

To make room for the essential

And over time

As boulder is smashed into rock

Pounded into dirt

Mixed with dung

To become

Soil teeming with life

Finally songs rise from a garden

New gestures emerge and live

In recognition of the difficulty that was

And they are louder more boisterous and sensational

As they must be.

When our ancestors rushed in and

Crossed the Red River they

Hardly noticed the billboard which says

Abandon hope all ye who enter here.

Accidentally obedient they in fact

Did not *hope*

They acted

They did not play *let's pretend*

But their grandchildren built the Wortham

And the Tobin Center

And today imagine a future that is even more bountiful

If we can dodge the hurricanes.

So when on your ten-hour highway pilgrimage to see

That 60,000 square foot gun range in Midland

You enter a hotel room sized toilet stall

While 100 pumps refuel massive SUVs outside

Remember that there are reasons why

The King Ranch is larger than Rhode Island

That Beaumont is home to the world's largest fire hydrant

A Cyclops' giant sculpted eye watches downtown Dallas

And that Amarillo has both a 72-ounce steak

And a 24-inch wide cheeseburger.

III

He wore that ring across the fruited plain

Through loss and grief he shouldered wounds and pain

Four score and ten that weighty ring he bore

Engraved with "honor" his mother's word he wore

With thigh pierced shoulder ripped ankle smashed

He soldiered on until the final lash

Governor general always eager to create

Upward trajectory surely seemed his fate

A fleeting retreating marriage personal shame

He escaped to Cherokess to avoid the blame

With tears he helped them in their forced trek west

Impossible situation he did his best

Survival yes but almost all it cost

Much was preserved but so much more was lost

In the House with cane he delivered pain

A pistol misfired but "honor" maintained

To Texas unchained a new campaign

Embracing again the open terrain

Under post oak he sat ankle shot

The surrender he accepted with tranquil heart

If time here could forever and always cease

He led the Republic and always strove for peace

Lamar the poet followed but war he made

Promises broken Chief Bowles now dead

But Houston undaunted led us to union

From there "honor" forbade dissolution

The flag was lowered and a new one raised

Sun set on the Republic - Texas became a State

To Congress and the Senate Houston returned

In time the war drums began to churn

Calhoun's ghost boasted of secession

In vain attempt was Houston's intercession

Union man the Governor could not commit

To take the oath would make him counterfeit

The Southern cause he alone could see was lost

Complete simplicity almost all it cost

The Letters came General Johnston passed

Grieving alone living as an outcast

Internal exile he stayed and watched and wept

Losses real but always "honor" kept

Sorrows full with Homeric strife he did fly

Some glories won but sorrows piled high

Pope's *Iliad* was played out in him and through him

Who would choose to go this way again?

Though strife and mourning and rejection marks his years

But yet his work endures and Texas lives

At Steamboat House his saga drew to close

Old wounds grew numb his breathing slowed

Memories and impressions recalled events of life

Then twice he called for his place and for his wife

But no more work for Texas could be made

And peaceful slept the mighty Houston's shade

IV

And the black-and-white wooden arms drop bob and bounce

bells clang hypnosis-inducing red strobe lights pulse back

and forth and your headlights briefly illuminate boxcars

speeding by and the bells are drowned out by the monotone

churning rhythmic racket noise light motion until the last car

whizzes past shrinks gracefully dissolving into the purple

night-distance and you wonder briefly what happened to

cabooses as you shift back into drive grip the wheel ten and

two and again the bells magnetically pull the arms up like a

drawbridge on the Thames but fast the quiet comes the bells

stop the arms wobble into their vertical salute-rest trucks

facing you cross and as you tug your trailer over those

railroad tracks in Krum, a crossroads and hub of past present

and future your Texas freedom-journey to a new place begins

Perceptions once taken become memories

Then the processing begins

Your memories meld with others in ceremony and dance

Or collision random encounters and jumbles

Conversations liturgy pie fights letters

Novels scrums banquets skirmishes sucker punches

Out of these bubbling cauldrons

Shared mythologies songs and tales rise

Until they expire and fall unrenewed by the wayside

And that is when you load up your

Remaining possessions and cart them

To the other side of the tracks

Then keep going one way or the other

To the city

Or to the country

Or back again

Your freedom-journey grail-quest continues.

If you miss cultivating a garden like your grandmother

Maintaining her sourdough starter

Named Moses (or was it Noah?)

You will see traffic as toxic and

Like an exile in Babylon long for a return to the old world

If you look into a dusty open field

See emptiness only and

Dream of Shakespeare's Globe

Vietnamese food and Tiffany's

You will need living bodies chattering opinions

Twinkling city-lights

A place where car horns in traffic

Form an orchestral brass section.

Either city or country may be freedom or servitude

Both can be chaos dead end

Stifling sweltering stagnant suffocating

Waste lands

Do you remember the box of peaches and the pie?

Or do you remember the worm?

Your answer will decide your trajectory

But hear this:

The choice is not city or country

The choice is despair or life

Boredom or flourishing

Stagnation or vivacity

Action or tedium

Slow death or freedom

Preference matters but no place will magically rescue you.

Whatever order and meaning and life we impart

To a place and with a people

A life of significant soil

Endures only with constant imaginative re-infusing

Of understanding context gratitude and joy

We bathe our days with purposeful action

Observation explanation and vigor

Or else we die.

From your lofty highchair perch

You study the sunlight pattern on the floor

Descend and move between the table legs

Explore your world open cabinets

With lightning speed weave in and out of

Shadowy corners and corridors

Advance boldly into your yard

Even beyond your curb

As you do the world becomes stranger

More difficult to understand

The heavy burden of the growing soul perplexes and offends

Just so we learn to cope

But our coping may require us to move

From one place to another

Perhaps that new place

Should be Texas

Our metropolises cities towns

Villages farms ranches and ghost towns

And here begin again

Your new home our vast land

To stake your claim

For your longed for freedom-future

Do you feel the call?

Is yours a remembered and felt

Lush primordial past like Austin's Edenic euphoric visions?

Or a future powered by nuclear fusion robotic humming

Techno-commerce strategic equity raises and

Seamless high-tech garments

Resembling the bioluminescence of jellyfish?

Or is it simple direct tactile and personal

    The smell of fresh cut grass

Post-midnight blues gig intermission cigarette smoke

A pumpkin on the vine growing daily oranger

The satisfying fat sizzle-drip onto red oak coals

Hot brass dropping to the ground

Food truck grub and steel guitar twang

The mingling of malt Dripping Springs copper vats and Time?

Texas

A place and a people

Where we are and where we go

To adapt and dream and mix and create

To remember project attempt

Suffer design speculate

Agree disagree share plow cultivate

Cooperate compete drill flourish

Try fail renew harvest innovate

Gather connect push pull

And build

Freely

And an imported turkey-red carpet that is the talk of the town brightens the oak-and-brass trimmed reception hall of a fine old hotel in what used to be called Deep Elm or just Central Track because of the Houston and Texas Central Railroad but is now called Deep Ellum and here Freedmen and European immigrants built cotton gins brick warehouses a Ford Model T plant and then came the music blues and jazz and the night life and the artists and as quickly as it came the railroad left and the Central Expressway bisected Deep Ellum but the musical ghosts and echoes lingered and newer music followed even Nirvana gigged here the continually painted tunnel was here now gone but spread throughout this beehive-neighborhood where you can get tattooed after midnight meeting mingling creating nourishing a crossroads and hub of past present and future your Texas freedom-journey continues

V

Distilled and condensed

Weighty abstractions

Words loaded with generational

Nuance flavor and vitality

We speak of *freedom*

Internal music swells

Images cascade before us

Our breathe quickens

We nod and blink away excess moisture

Swallow and grip the hammer a bit tighter

Assuming others feel the same

And then today ends

But if tomorrow we fail to act freely

Our red wine turns brackish brown

Accretion slips into rot

The finest peppery Tuscan olive oil

Begins to smell like crayons

And the accumulated patina of *freedom* dulls

If we

Stop experimentally sculpting with found rusty screws

And Pabst Blue Ribbon cans

Forget that Myrtis Dightman from Crockett did more

Than hang on for eight seconds

Ignore the mountain pass echo-scream

Of the solitary eagle

Grow squeamish at an airport with the words

"I need to declare a firearm"

Avoid grime sweat and callous and seek clinical sterility

Play along half-etherized with sinister rigged rules

Fail to applaud things well done

Prefer empty shiny cold steel carts in disinfected hallways to

Cedar plant boxes bursting with soil manure and life

If we

Sloganeer rather than reason and persuade

Cower in fear terrorized by unseen germs

Empower fake-yellow fluorescent light and lying rancid rituals

Pretend that cheap perfumes chemically mask death-stench

Display a "Workers of the World Unite!" sign in

Our game processing shop

Then our abstraction *freedom*

Melts like an abandoned ice sculpture

A generalized puddle of nothingness

Lilt becomes slurry sludge

A brown mess of metaphysical meaninglessness

A lifeless insipid slogan shape without form

Tepid water and generic instant coffee in Styrofoam

Dry cicada carcass in a deserted orchard

Blank wall

In a gutted farmhouse

In a windy hollow

As far away as Byzantium

But

If we

Move create act

Imagine a future that is impressionistic yet distinct

With power and resources

Fire intrinsic motivation

Nurture without exploiting

Not losing focus on small-minded pursuits and

Instantaneous gratification

Resist sloth despair pettiness distracting bits of paper

But wait on and with care bring that future into part of now

Accepting joyfully the constraints that are

While imagining what could be next and tomorrow

And by faith *believe* the Word of the Lord

That if we now cast our net on the other side of the boat

Nourishing abundance and

Freedom

will follow

FARWELL

O Röschen rot!

Der Mensch liegt in größter Not!

Der Mensch liegt in größter Pein!

Je lieber möcht' ich im Himmel sein.

Da kam ich auf einen breiten Weg:

Da kam ein Engelein und wollt' mich abweisen.

Ach nein! Ich ließ mich nicht abweisen!

Ich bin von Gott und will wieder zu Gott!

Der liebe Gott wird mir ein Lichtchen geben,

Wird leuchten mir bis in das ewig selig Leben!

"Urlicht" from _Des Knaben Wunderhorn_

People exploit what they have merely concluded to be of value, but they defend what they love, and to defend what we love we need a particularising language, for we love what we particularly know.

Wendell Berry, _Life Is A Miracle: An Essay Against Modern Superstition_

The leader of the troop unlocked his word-hoard...

Beowulf, lines 258-259; Seamus Heaney translation

In the sweat of thy face shalt thou eat bread, till thou return unto the ground; for out of it wast thou taken: for dust thou art, and unto dust shalt thou return.

Genesis 3:19

"Imagine getting killed by an arrow in this day and age," Augustus said. "It's ridiculous, especially since they shot at us fifty times with modern weapons and did no harm."

"You always was careless," Call said. "Pea said you rode over a hill and right into them. I've warned you about that very thing a thousand times. There's a better ways to approach a hill."

"Yes, but I like being free on the earth," Augustus said. "I'll cross the hills where I please."

Larry McMurtry, _Lonesome Dove_

I

I am from God and shall return to God

The desert reclaims the Sears Roebuck ranch house

Our bodies die but will mysteriously return

So something always *is*

Love is what creates and endures and

The love that moves the sun and the other stars is

Forever coming and going

Diminishing and enduring but never failing

Our language digs deep into the dirt and remembers

The tribal vengeful unforgetting blood-feuding heroics and the

Loyalty generosity and unhesitating rhythmic

Fearlessness of Anglo-Saxon

Our language also ascends by Norman French

Upwards through higher concepts

Romantic noble cosmopolitan universal even speculative

But ascends only so high as we remain tethered here

We struggle to say what we mean and mean what we say

We want our yes and no to ring with clarity and certainty

But mostly we get stuck with that's not what I meant at all

Yet there is grace and poetry and when that fails

There is music

And when music fails

There is silence

And touch

    She takes his hand

    It's quiet uptown

Even as we ascend

Erratically yet inexorably to the Word

We mingle here in the dirt and sand

With spear-shaped leeks and amber

And with sledge-hammer

Pounding big rocks into little rocks

Sifting and hoeing with words

Panning for truths

In this dust there is truth

But the process is dirty

I am from God and shall return to God

II

Conquest

The Acheans bury Troy

The tractor displaces the horse-plow

Fleeing Trojans invade Italy and overrun the Rutuli

Fire-breathing railroads swoop over meandering river barges

In the rush to the Gulf of Mexico

Brutus of Troy slays the last of the giants in Britain

Badged Big Bend park rangers wield pencil document and

Officialdom and replace unbadged ranchers

The Romans flee Britain

The Angles Saxons and Jutes arrive

Land stolen borrowed cultivated and abandoned

Irrepressible Celts resist English Civil War and Cromwell

The westward splash-rush across ocean

Fleeing Puritans and tobacco farmers

The Spanish Moscoso Expedition brings breeding

Infesting and roaming mustangs to Texas

And their claimed Wild Horse Desert on the map

Is bigger than most European countries

The resolute march to the Pacific

Railroad tie-laying land surveying

Sharp-axe wielding pioneers

Walt Whitman verse ringing in their ears

Longhorns dispossess buffalo one for one

Comanches perfect horsemanship and High Plains warfare

Old Man Goodnight fences Palo Duro Canyon and

Introduces the Hereford

Jumano ousted by the mighty Apache

Only to be defeated by mightier Comanche

Normans cross cascading waves in 1066

Chaucer's language is born

Comancheria

Pax Romana ends with invasions from the East

The Karankawa hold back the French for a time

The Road goes ever on and on

And there were giants in the earth in those days

Mighty men which were of old, men of renown

Peace

peasants trembling emerge from thatched cottages as
smoke clears

and hear

the piano player in the saloon again play a familiar song
recalling the old country and emancipation proclaimed out
loud in Galveston

and see

Moses descend from Mount Sinai countenance ablaze

and read

that sixty Texans declared independence and that public hangings may no longer spontaneously rectify crimes just committed

and remember

when the War Dance incited but now memorializes

Vikings exhausted settle for the long winter mount tractors in spring and after breakfast head into town for feed and diesel

and hear

on the radio how Romeo and Juliet ignored blood-feuds and leapt over shield-walls

and see

the Jets and Sharks hoist Tony overhead as Maria solemnly joins the procession

and read

to their children the story of Joshua Houston's freedom journey and how his son Samuel Walker Houston is buried in Oakwood in Huntsville near the General

and remember

that we have survived five oil crashes or maybe ten

lonely monastic scriveners of the Texas and Red River
Telegraph Company convert faint wire-signals into ink on
paper

and hear

tale of an immigrant courier of literacy riding up in a dust
cloud to a clapboard schoolhouse of red cedar planks
furnished with barely bound yellow pages

and see

fire tamed candles lit asphalt spread and smoky beds of oak
coals tended overnight

and read

of the arrival of a printing press in Galveston from Baltimore
and of those chroniclers who first wielded the magic of voice
without sound

and remember

the scribbling scribes who designed land recordation
systems illuminated as-builts for that new bread factory in

Big Spring drafted building codes and hurricane evacuation
plans

fifty-nine believing immortals set the cornerstone for Lovett
Hall in hope for what was yet to be

and hear

sword-clash converting into the rhythmic minting of coin
and then the Mesquite Symphony percussion section

and see

crop dusters daringly and noisily spraying pesticide for locals
in the summer of '47

and read

in their Book of Kells that Simon has become Peter and for
freedom Christ died for us

and remember

learning from the Lubbock Avalanche Journal that Buddy
Holly died in that plane crash but in the Lamb County Leader
that Waylon Jennings did not

drone operators from Texas Tech conduct recon missions to power precision plant phenotyping and crop ecophysiology

and hear

of Oracle's acquisitions and the native Texas stubbornness of George Mitchell injecting fluid and sand down a well breaking rock and releasing trapped energy and power

and see

Michael Debakey gliding from MASH unit to roller pump to sewing Dacron and laboring at the cardiovascular surgery table

and read

that Pantex now only disassembles weapons that Tesla will build the Cybertruck in Austin and of synthetic rubber lithium-ion battery components seismic imaging and thermo-sensitive scaffolding systems for lab-grown brisket

and remember

the multitudes given more life by MD Anderson's proton therapy center

and smell

nostril-burning Normandy gun powder of our grandfathers
fusing seamlessly with fragrant and savory Fourth of July
fireworks of our grandchildren

and feel

paid-work callous merging indistinguishably with forced-
work callous

and taste

caldo de res from the Texas Farm Bureau's recipe

and see

that the Lord is good

until the luxury of boredom

sets in

and the once mighty empire *Comancheria* shrinks to an
annual pow-wow in Lawton, Oklahoma

Memory

On the lowest level of the hand-hewn bookshelf sits a spiky mess, a leaning full meter tower-pile of paper: a jumbled mound of parchment, newspaper, manuscript, survey, bond paper; love letter, music notation pad, butcher paper, stock certificate, coloring book; hard drive, sizzle reel, index card and Christmas wrap.

Near the bottom of the stack, loosely swaddled in thinning disintegrating cellophane are the opening pages of Herodotus' *Histories* where he inquires and records and fabricates so that Greek and barbarian, conqueror and conquered, might attain a measure of glory and not be forgotten for great and marvelous deeds.

In the middle of the stack, a single cassette tape sits tucked between two jaundiced flaky magazines. Speakers recount the vivid memory that freedom meant at first being let loose like a rabbit into the woods: terrifying, uncertain, disorienting. Owning nothing except their labor and their skills, which they could now sell, they were, strangely, free. Things were new. And some of those that previously forced them to work, were now paying.

Some of the newly free moved to find this paying work. Many a grandfather came over onto this other side of the river. Hamilton County did not allow freedmen, but Coryell County did. So the freedmen walked. Like so many in Texas history, they just walked. They walked until they could freely raise a barn, arm themselves, take last names, elect a mayor and start a school.

Stories of victors tend to rise to the top of the stack. But like Herodotus, we do well at dusk as streetlights warm and the bonfire stirs to life like an ancient volcano, to remember with ink and pen, guitar and harmonica; with blackeyed pea and collard green; with perfume, linen and old leather, the silent submission and endurance of those in our memory stream who were conquered for a time, and suffered, and might be forgotten, and to sing of those who walked to freedom.

We also do well to remember those who never submitted.

III

Aberdeen-Angus

Angel of Goliad

Archer City bookstores

Alamo

Armadillos

Amarillo by Morning

Born on the Island

Blue Topaz

Beef brisket

Blue skies

Barbed wire

Blue Bell

Bullfrogs

Buccee's

Burnt orange Longhorns

Barbacoa

Chili con carne

Cowboy churches

Cinco de Mayo

Chewy prailines

Chip and Joanna

Chips and salsa

Daingerfield Tigers 1985

Dandelions

Eagle Hollow

East Black Hills

Friday night lights

Forney Jackrabbits

Gruene Hall

Guacamole

Gulf Coast Oysters

Guadalupe sea bass

Garage sales	Geronimo
Hereford	Horned toads
Hobby Center	Horseflies
Independence Baptist Church	Indian Creek
Juneteenth	Jackson Creek
Jesse Jones	Jones Creek
King Ranch	Kyle Field
Killen's	K-Bar Ranch
Lost San Saba Silver Mine	Love Field
Monarch butterfly	Mockingbirds
Margaret McDermott Bridge	Mineral Wells
Naps on Sunday	Noonday
Orange Grove	Oldham County
Pecan trees	Pine Curtain
Pennzoil Place	Prada Marfa
Quanah	Quail season

Rice Hotel	Ranchitos Las Lomas
Ruby red grapefruit	Rattlesnake round ups
Road kill	Rothko Chapel
Sweet tea	Spindletop
Sighting scopes	San Jacinto Day
Sus scrofa	Sage in bloom
Seminole bats	Swamp rabbits
Terlingua	Tiki Island
Tumbleweeds	Tornadoes
Union Grove	Uvalde
Vaqueros	Val Verde County
Van Cliburn Piano Competition	Von Ormy
White limestone	White-tail deer
Willie Waylon	Waggoner Ranch
Whataburger Bible studies	West Texas Intermediate
Williams Tower	Whiteface

XIT	Xanna Indians
Ygnacio Creek	Yellow Rose
Zavala	Zapata County

IV

The Ten

Just a-gleaming in the sun and a-howling at the moon

Resolute

Stark

Brittle

Honest

Weird

Nude

They have no secrets

They just lean

In formation

Into the wind

Not exactly defiant

But certainly not compliant

A bit lonely, their glory faded, but with the patina of nostalgia

A whiff of post-war abundance and optimism.

Before them

The Comanches bivouacked, marauded and danced

The ranchers followed and tarried a bit longer

Fencing and grazing

Then farmers seeded and harvested

Speculators gambled and railroads bullied

Then came Armageddon, the arid paint-peeling

Suffocating dust of the 1930s

Like all the other nomads that came and went before them

The Ten are neither at home nor out of place

Like a Route 66 gas station and our great grandparents

They too will slowly dissolve into the background

Obscured by the perpetual motion of endless, gritty wind

But for now, they continue with their business

Not noticing you, but allowing you to notice them

Tough, but not invulnerable

Resilient, but hardly immortal

Weeds tumble and bounce

Coffee cools

Rust sets in

Tears fall and dry

Tailfins disappear

So many Baptists and so many others

Gather here together to paint, to hope and to dream and keep moving with the wind

They also stop by to paint

To recall

To accept

And hold their heads high like the Cadillacs

V

Sharp metal barbs twisted together

Wrapped around a wire strand

Light as air stronger than whiskey cheap as dirt

Our Treaty of Versailles before there was one

With now fenced and staked claims

Dust settled and stampedes ceased

The rhythm of hoof beats along

Wind-scoured lightning-scorched prairie trail

Gave way to a settled and civilized cycle

Of sun and moon moving in time

Above a defined grazing place and rotating seasons

Our technology-driven shortcut to new

World-changing map lines

There's little safety in maps

What one pencil and ruler gave

A cheap rubber eraser takes away

Battalions of men and boys have perished

Because a general

Drew a line on a field map

And the light was dim

Ancient river-borders with real authority separate us from

Oklahoma, Mexico and some of Louisiana

While an invisible and arbitrary designation

Divides time itself and delineates us from

New Mexico without even pretending

Physical or metaphysical rationale

We could treat that border like the wind does

But we imagine it an impenetrable Great Wall of China

And thus people grew up Full Texan in

Texline Glenrio and Farwell

Even as they daily looked out their back window

Across State Line Road and stared into the

Flat brown barrenness beyond Texas

And back into the previous hour

What if through expressionless bureaucratic idolatry

For boxes checked and unchecked

Or court room theatrics or just good old-fashioned conquest

That north-south line moved east just a few miles

Bringing down the solitary star and raising the Zia red sun

Over these border towns?

Did everything that happened there previously

Then retroactively happen an hour earlier?

Did we grow up facing the wrong direction?

Are we now from New Mexico?

Is our identity as untethered as the ubiquitous

Tumbleweeds we rarely noticed?

Are we all just less intense versions of Cynthia Ann Parker?

Our memories like our spaces are vast violent and
fluctuating

Your sense impressions and recollections

Of Laredo Lowriders (and the jalapeño festival)

Ft. Worth Stockyards or Jacob's Dream in Abilene

Or Prada Marfa

Will not be the same as someone else's

And your future recollections will differ

From your recollections today

Past present and future are slippery movable and transient

We weave through history places people names things

We don't discover history it discovers us

Our forefathers ate cactus and dandelion greens

Because they had to

Today we enter our prickly pear preserves in county fairs and

Willingly choose superfood salads off a menu

And just so we realize we are not alone

And these journeys take a lifetime

Fortifying our memories (and thus our present) in solitude

We forge our future together in action

A blue and white Leyland 245 bringer of truth and life

Scrapes grunts and wheezes and with scratch sputter and fret

Rids a patch of rash sweet-gum dreaming of future seasons

But spares wise oaks and reveals a roof of sky and star-leaves

A half-light canopy for the emerging grass ground-net

In the clear pasture just beyond the tree line with a prayer

And a shoulder shrug we invite a bluebonnet chorus to live

Inscrutable yet reliable like a Gulf Coast inlet

During hurricane season going where they will without reason

We know even the sturdiest live oak can die that bees

Leave and that a galvanized wire stapled and set

Deep into a cedar fence post rots with rust but we still pray

Fully aware of coming drift leakage and wreckage yet alive

By saw scythe plow anvil and hammer-sweat

Over a year of dusty thumb-busting bug-bitten evenings

We tilt that westerly facing porch to the south 23 degrees

Capture the still point find freedom and gaze on daily sunset

The angle blunts August's dogmatism and imprecatory prayer

And embraces silent February's sunny prelude to renewed life

Forever daily watching the weaving of future quartet vignette

A blending palette at days end a song cycle of life-seasons

Crimson blood-intensity leaden grey lonely ice blue freeze

Blueberry peach crisp lemon yes! withering emerald regret

Evening embrace of life as lived renewed by evening prayer

Harmony discord change violence death birth and life

The oldest pick up will carry us over the roughest roads yet

Heavy evenings soft mornings burnt out ends of smoky days

Embrace the storm fare forward brew coffee ride the breeze

Clear a forest path line it with stacked limestone parapet

And remember our grandchildren in prayer

THE BRAZOS DE RIOS

A whole river is mountain country and hill country and flat country and swamp and delta country, is rock bottom and sand bottom and weed bottom and mud bottom, is blue, green, red, clear, brown, wide, narrow, fast, slow, clean, and filthy water, is all kinds of trees and grasses and all the breeds of animals and birds and men that pertain and have ever pertained to its changing shores, is a thousand differing and not compatible things in-between that point where enough of the highland drainlets have trickled together to form it, and that wide, flat, probably desolate place where it discharges itself into the salt of the sea.

John Graves, *Goodbye to a River*

That night Augustus stopped to rest his horse, making a cold camp on a little bluff and eating some jerky he had brought along. He was in the scrubby post-oak country near the

Brazos and from his bluff could see far across the moonlit valleys.

Larry McMurtry, *Lonesome Dove*

I sat upon the shore

Fishing, with the arid plain behind me

Shall I at least set my lands in order?

London Bridge is falling down falling down falling down

Poi s'ascose nel foco che gli affina

Quando fiam uti chelidon – O swallow swallow

Le Prince d'Aquitaine a' la tour abolie

These fragments I have shored against my ruins

T.S. Eliot, *The Waste Land*

And all the Israelites passed over on dry ground, until all the people were passed clean over Jordan.

Joshua 3:17

I

Hushed, expectant in the sun-kissed

Afternoon living room

Our great-grandparents twirl

The wavelength knob on the family's oversized radio

And through the pop and crackle-sparks

Sample a medley of voices:

Dallas Houston Tyler Abilene McAllen El Paso Amarillo

Morsels of music, snatches of news

Commodity prices, weather and rants

Thunderings of J. Frank Norris and lesser Baptist shouters

Seasoned with King James

Or Bob Wills, fiddler and bandleader, racy and joyous

Marrying hillbilly melodies and hot jazz

And still the king

Or the fusion of the two

Pass the Biscuits Pappy, generously serving up

Western swing, the Ten Commandments and the Bible

From the back of a fast-moving car

Tight grip in our hand at a restaurant

Workspace restroom grocery store line red light

We jostle glance hop tweet nudge stall pinch swipe forward

We upsize and downsize

Leave toss rearrange cancel replace

Did you forget? She grew up here

Did you even know? This soil bedeviled our ancestors and

Might nourish our descendants

Can you not see? There used to be right here a church and a

Saloon with a shared piano

But do you hear? The deep music-echo from the earth

Its constants, its continual support:

    Advancing and flowing

    Widening and deepening

Pushing and pulling

Drying and shrinking

Roaming and remaining

Leaving and abiding

A River never remembers

Because it never forgets

It knows no past

Source and mouth together always now

Always present always changing

Always ancient always new

Gustav Mahler said a symphony must contain the world

He might have said the same about a River

Containing *andante furioso legato pianissimo staccato*

Der Ring des Niebelungen begins and ends with the Rhine

Nile Yangtze Congo Amazon Thames The Mighty Mississip

These great rivers stretch their music away across the earth

But The Brazos is peculiarly ours

Its melody, like family, continually

    Building and decaying

    Delighting and disappointing

    Disclosing and hiding

    Confusing and convincing

    Delivering and evading

    Rising and falling

A River transports antique source-myths

Into now and tomorrow and that is well-known

But a River also ferries slivers of ginger

Drizzles of orange and dollops of honey

Local morsels for a particular people

We don't exactly know

Old Hannah and Old Shine

But yet we do

Half-forgotten half-fabricated half-exaggerated

These conjured impressions resonate

And the old prison work song

Confirms our togetherness along the banks of The River:

    Ain't no more cane on The Brazos

    It's all been ground down to molasses

Our never-frozen enigmatic conniving crescent

Our life- and death-force

The Brazos

Snakes mythologizes and relentlessly composes

From the High Plains through

Canyon grass shrub hill and forest

Before its slow salty conclusion in

The Gulf of Mexico

Ready with its wind arms and

Dead beat bird calls

Perhaps our waters don't compare to other Rivers

But we have our song to sing

A beginning and an end and an *intermezzo*:

Jagged, hopeful men

High on the dream of independence declared

At Washington-on-the-Brazos

Built and built again

A hardscrabble Capitol of whiskey-breath

Poker games and livestock

By the dusky molten bronze River

Singing low, they dug deep

A vision of their own and gathered together

To forget the dying spirit of soldiers

Scurrying south towards their Mexican homes and

To remember a free future yet to be

Until their tired bones

Dulled by the lotus-lush Eden, the rolling perfection

And the *La Bahia* pecan

Spurned sense and change and let

The railroad pass them by

A short fluttering descent to town

And then to village

Able men and future taken

By the time they realized their mistake

A final fiery insult consumed

The abandoned wood-frame buildings remaining

The very place where freedom began

The ghost of the town char and dust

But The River, muddy and wise, sings still

Like the decay of chapter one of our freedom-story

The source of our longest river

Shifts elusively leaving a dry remnant

A dusty ditch where mermaids sing no more:

A highway 84 sign today bends to the dirt

That once promised more

Yellow House Draw is only a memory

And barely that

Yet as origins become continually and beautifully obscured

And contributing tributaries tangled

The accumulated memories are here concentrated into a great

Joy of a cappella blue-water clarity:

> As I went down in the river to pray
> Studying about that good ol' way
> And who shall wear the starry crown
> Good Lord, show me the way

In the early days, The Brazos

Sometimes sleepy, sometimes with a wakefulness

Sped by cutting the land

Confusing its new tenants

Texans yet to learn its ways

We know better now: our River ricochets

Swerves and changes course

Going where it wants

A mirror of its people

Using and destroying what it needs before

Settling into a slow new easy

Blues ballad routine

For a time

But who knows for how long?

Trusting, we follow our founders and settle on its banks

Plant trees and hope of future

Flourishing spring entanglements of

Wind branches birds sunlight and shadow blossom and fruit

Until one stormy Memorial Day you go onto the porch

With a cup of coffee and see

The River risen

Familiar trees and Longhorn Road vanished

The house that someone grew up in

On Buckskin Road near Simonton

Teetering foundationless condemned

On the edge of this, our ancient River

Silently singing a new history

Revealing its many faces

Brown blue rough smooth

The song more complex human complete

Bulls cooperate each fall to load into a trailer

To go to a field and begin the cycle of birth and spring renewal

Between Possum Kingdom and Waco dammed and controlled

The Brazos is corralled into thirst-quenching irrigation

For miles its waters run clean, blue and navigable

New wetlands bring rest for migrating geese

While rice paddies flourish in Brazoria County

Levees protect sugarcane fields in Sugar Land

And magnesium in Freeport flows from its waters

We think we have won the earth

Having reclassified assets and liabilities

On the balance sheet with pencil and eraser

But really we are hoping faintly

Alongside forces we fail to understand

And when the bull refuses cooperation

Like Achilles fighting Xanthus the river god

With our Wagnerian hammer strikes

We drive scores of concrete columns

Into the Fort Bend County earth and beg

The Brazos to stop its erosion

The taste of iron and smell of concrete in the air

From this battle royal eventually

A sort of peace treaty emerges

But who knows for how long?

The River sings

A permanent thing though never stagnant

Our Dante – or at least our Virgil

Our companion and guide

Always present always changing

Always ancient always new

II

In what world is eight seconds a fundamental

Measurement of time?

And where ten-yard increments

Measure the span between life and death?

Where crossing the Sabine going west

A sign says 857 miles to El Paso and that

Seems not only relevant but a bargain?

The answer is in our world where otherwise arbitrary spots

Are fenced and defined and then infused

With life

Common language story-telling action living liturgy

So long as the music lasts

And you are the music while the music lasts

The lines between cooperation

Persuasion and coercion are often

Dulled gray and mostly not lines at all but zones

And our recognition lags behind our arrival

Even so over here

You have Xerxes lashing the Hellespont

While over here

You have children playing house like the olden days

in a sturdy gray shed built by grandfather

while grandmother within ear shot

paints *en plein air* from

an even older photograph and

tells how their mothers

played in that same shed

which was red then

A commonly-held stretch of The Brazos altered by the WPA

Creates a deep placid reservoir for

Crystal-clear canoeing beneath emerging cliffs

Surrounded by craggy banks

Now

A place to host mossy-green slippery boat ramps

Meat-and-sand picnics and

Camping trips rendered memorable through intense
discomfort:

Remember the snap of the rope-swing?

Remember how prickly and itchy our sunburns felt?

Remember how I told you we would need a rain fly?

If after midnight you squint and peer

Through the spiny shadowy shroud of

Ashe juniper trees and mesquite

You will see around the campfire boys hitting each other

Smell undercooked sausages burnt marshmallows

And hear a youth pastor on acoustic guitar

At dawn heat and silence rise and

The dance with our grandparents and our grandchildren

Mediated across generations continues

Though awkward hesitant broken fumbling

Failing to say what we mean and mean what we say

Faltering and forgetting

Still

This is the dance

And occasionally even a balter

An aquifer of life

An Ogallala an Edwards

Surrounded by sand silt clay and gravel

Still

This deep music of the dance runs beneath and through us

Unseen unheard

The powerful flowing stillness

Between lightning and thunder

The time between two simultaneous events

Nourishing electrified felt

We are here

In our beginning

III

You can grasp your section of a river

Comprehend it and know it even master it

Like a Comanche warrior on the High Plains

With only wind and sky-map

Knowing where the next watering hole lies hidden

It is possible to know your section of The River

And know it well

Before 1869 crossing The Brazos

In Waco was impossibly dangerous

As the Chisholm Trail grew in importance

This crossing became essential

So the local Masons proposed of all things

A suspension bridge

A marvel of engineering

Three million locally fired bricks

Soon to be cousin of the Brooklyn Bridge

Before Dr Pepper and Baylor came to town

Even by Texas standards

Waco was remote:

The nearest railroad a century of miles away

So supplies were loaded onto a steamer in Galveston

Ferried to Bryan, then piled into ox-pulled covered wagons

And dragged over a pothole-filled dirt road

Roman technology two millennia old had not made it to
Texas

Even so

Problem solved constraint circumvented

With those materials

They built the two-lane suspension bridge

Wide enough for stagecoaches to pass each other

Or for Longhorns to flow across one side

And walkers on the other

Then began the long procession of thousands

Cable-arms now lifting care-encumbered or hope-filled drivers

So many

Inhaling and exhaling

Each bearing a burden of sorrow-eyes fixed to feet downcast

Or hope of riches and future eyes lifted elated

Or both

Access now to distant markets horizon and sky

Forgotten below

The Brazos slips by ignored but unoffended

When internal combustion fired motor vehicles

Found their way to Texas

They also crossed The Brazos

Tolls were collected and the bridge paid for

After a century

The bridge was retired to walkers only

And by the 1980s became a place

Where even Baptists could dance

And gamble by tossing tortillas onto an abandoned pier

A game of skill and chance

Problem solved constraint circumvented

The building and destruction of bridges

Can begin and end wars

Perhaps because The River has said

These two parts should not be connected

A bridge is a thing of consequence

But eventually The River will outlast our temporary pretension

At least at this crossing

You can now traverse The Brazos by foot on the Baylor campus

And enter the Coliseum

Pass a bronze statue of our Hercules

Deep underneath someday a Heinrich Schliemann

From the Texas Hill Country

Will find the shards of the apartment The Island

And conjure tales of a past now buried

We cross to the other side of a river

And we build bridges

So that others may follow

Leaving behind some things that need to be left

And faring forward to places we need to go

But here is a truth:

We also burn bridges

Sometimes bridges are burned from under us

And this is also a truth:

Though London bridge burned

They rebuilt London bridge.

They built that bridge again.

IV

Have you ever tried to photograph

The shifting purple-skirts curtaining the

Rippling crimson enveloping the yellow

The patchwork layered quilt of impenetrable

Denim cotton-clouds and vast expanses of

Blue-gray wispy nothingness

The continuous celestial mellow movement of

Light-color and growing shadow

The movement of today from now to memory?

Trying to photograph the sunset is like

Trying to watch the wings of a hummingbird

Or precisely define the late October drop in temperature

    Surprising and familiar

    Do you feel that?

But yet

There is a time for an old photograph

Even of a sunset and for clicking on the memory folder

To remind you that you were there

The dry secure embedded stone on

The River bank where you gather your footing and

Wade into the living stream of memory

    Do you remember that chocolate sauce?

    Why did he think that she would find that funny?

    Did you think he would make that shot?

    Remember how silent it was and then the baby cried?

And further yet

Some photos contain more truth

Than we can know because

We can only take so much reality

They radiate across oceans disregarding borders

Instantly inciting longing for and into

A remembered and imagined future

Some images set eternity into motion

And call someone to step into The River

at a particular point

thus changing The River forever

In this new future some day she will look with her first born

and say

that it all began

for us

here

With this photograph

Quick now here now always

He said

      Words move, music moves only in time

Yes

We were placed into The River

Here

And our children today rightly

    Plot plan devour experiment and play

At NASA

Unaware of Challenger

This is the gift we give them

And the shock and pain of our Clear Lake friends

As fragments of Columbia scattered over East Texas

This is our burden to bear

Until they are ready

They will do the same for their children

Eventually we will

Step out of this River

Cross the River Jordan

To head to the Promised Land

Jordan

Yarden

Our physical descent from the snowy caps of Mount Hermon

Through the fertile vineyards and orchards below

And below further

To the lowest point on earth the Dead Sea

The way down is the way up

We will step out of *Yarden*

The ancient River where Jesus was baptized

    No chilling winds nor poisonous breath

    Can reach that healthful shore;

    Sickness, sorrow, pain and death,

    Are felt and feared no more

And cross over into Dante's River of Light

V

Animal paths become Indian paths become

Los Caminos Reales

Death in open country

Life along the road

No one denied no one assisted

Laughing parties of revelers

The steady march of fur and timber traders

Drunkards stagger couples elope highwaymen rob

Cottonwoods ghosts coyotes wind

Brown padres chanting move between Spanish missions

Boredom and isolation alongside heroic deeds

And even a few poems composed

Ruts hooves feet wagon wheels Goodyear tires

Shoed horses tracks trails roads hardened dirt to asphalt

The beating of this path took thousands of years

The River blinked once

LINCOLNVILLE

The mystic chords of memory, stretching from every battle-field, and patriot grave, to every living heart and hearthstone, all over this broad land, will yet swell the chorus...

Abraham Lincoln, *First Inaugural*

Of all that was done in the past, you eat the fruit, either rotten

    or ripe.

And the Church must be forever building,

and always decaying,

    and always being restored.

T.S. Eliot, *Choruses from "The Rock"*

Spring comes early down on the Esperanza. The mesquites were all in new leaf with that green so fresh and tender that the color seems to emanate into the sky. The bluebonnets and the pink phlox were sprinkling every hill and draw. The prickly pear was studded with waxy blossoms, and the glades were heavy with the perfume of white brush. It was a good season, and tallow weed and grass were coming together. It was time for the spring cow hunts and the putting up of herds for the annual drive north.

J. Frank Dobie, _The Longhorns_

"The favor I want from you will be my favor to you," Augustus said. "I want to be buried in Clara's orchard."

"In Nebraska?" Call asked, surprised. "I didn't see no orchard."

Augustus chuckled. "Not in Nebraska," he said. "In Texas, by that little grove of live oaks on the south Guadalupe." **Larry McMurtry, _Lonesome Dove_**

I

If you were to come here from Waco or from Houston

If you were to come here

From any place, from any where

You might think

You don't belong here

That you don't belong to us and we don't belong to you

We don't belong to anyone, we are free

And that is a way of putting it

But the greater reality surely is that we belong to Him

The Alpha and Omega

So we belong to each other

Not in ownership but in freedom and in all things human

Beautiful and painful tragic and comic eternal and temporal

It was for freedom Christ died for us

And it was for freedom that Texas was birthed

We belong to Texas

And Texas belongs to us

Few in number hearty in spirit

The newly free came here

Joining others brought here before

And settled here

On the west bank of the Leon River

Leaning on the everlasting arms

They farmed and sweated

Worked and prayed

In new-found liberty they built the

Bethlehem Baptist Church

On Sundays dressed and with or without shoes

They dashed and cut through the woods

To meet cousins at

The little wood and nail church house

Which was also a school

Bible drill preaching and singing

Babies asleep on a quilt pallet at the back

The slow meticulous march of civilization

Paid work land books family and neighbor

Integrating body tool soil and prayer

They loved the hills and hollows

Until the next generation

Moved to town and left the country

The older people died

The younger ones just moved out

In the midsummer heat somewhere

Between melting and boiling

They wander back to the old sanctuary

Finding trail markers along the way

Arriving just as the earth is turned

And sweet corn planted

Sodden seed stirs again to life

Green shoots weave upwards through

Dirt canopy and stretch and reach

For the blaze of life and heat above

Reunited here ever-morphing memories

Bubble to the surface

Dust blown off books

Old hot and savory pentatonic chords reverberate

The annual restatement of strong simple axioms of life

Yearly gathering of truth and weight in the life-giving heat

Even the blinding three o'clock

Glare of the longest day

Dissolves to dark merely warm

Humid breezeless evening and

Clicking cooling fans

Ice melts leaving diluted tea and lemon

The slow turning of the fabric of our days

The quiet cadence of holding and letting go

Creek becomes stream becomes trickle

And finally a dry riverbed

At room temperature

With each passing year faces grew fewer

Where is the summer, the bustling

Salty sweltering jubilant reunion?

Mighty deeds have become the saga of plain-spoken ghosts

Heroic verse recorded as oral history

Their words tumble forward and find hearing ears

And extend this Texas freedom journey

Quick now here now always

You are not here to romanticize, provoke resentment

Research scratch an itch

Fill in a missing line in your genealogy

You are here to kneel and meditate and see

The merger of prayer and life

And to taste a morsel of freedom

Until words then become flesh now and

Fuse generations

In liturgy of action

And Enoch walked with God: and he was not

For God took him

Though the dead no longer speaking

They still speak yet more clearly

Their words a Pentecostal fire

Which doesn't consume but builds

In ways different and beyond when they were alive

Here, the intersection of the timeless moment

Is Texas always and forever

II

Ash from the pit settles on a faded wrist tattoo

Recalling his service long ago, far away, that story ended

The ballet of smoke rises hovers and penetrates

Embers smolder

The dancing spectrum of the sunset unfolds

Blue turns to red turns to orange turns to pink

In a familiar timeless pattern

How many decades has he done this?

The day is done the work complete a chapter ends

Tomorrow his journey continues

Neither science nor art, more alchemy

Ancestral wisdom made immediate:

The wall scaled

King brisket on wax paper unadorned

Taste the sound of Lightnin' Hopkins blues

Behold the measured historic humanism

Of Elisabet Ney's sculptings

Savor the telling of Davy Crockett's tall tales

Taste and see that the Lord is good

The sounds of morning urban dawn

Light creeps over the horizon pavement warms

The smell of strong coffee and weak aftershave

Car doors close a block away

Redundant headlights power down

Traffic signals do my bidding

Cherishing the silence alone

I turn off the air conditioning

Listen to myself breathe and swallow and blink

Alone in that hour self-satisfied alone knowing that I alone

Will nab the familiar parking place

    Reach the top floor in the elevator alone.

But I met one walking, loitering and hurried

As I fixed upon that down-turned face

First-met stranger in the waning dusk

I caught the sudden look of three dead masters

Whom I had heard seen and read

But only half-recalled

One and many the shifting eyes of compound ghost

Recognizable yet unfamiliar

At the same time

Speechless and confused, I mustered: "Do I know you?"

Sort of like, "No español!"

Not really what I meant, but point made

And so, compliant to the common wind

Too strangely familiar for misunderstanding

In concord at this intersection time

Meeting here but nowhere again and for the first time

We shuffled in step together now across the

Parking garage pavement towards elevator

I said: "Why are you here? I don't deserve this."

My words echo

Thus in my mind

And they: "Let us disclose to you here, today, some wisdom.

You can cope with life through reputation

The well-told tall tale and martyrdom

Or through the blues or through

The elements of the songs

The whiskey and the smoke

Or through sculpture

The act of bringing something from the mind

Into our three-dimensions

But coping is not reconciliation

Nor is it redemption

It doesn't cleanse us

Because like Lady MacBeth

We can't wash

The spot out

For that you must seek

Your own salvation

With fear and trembling

But yet you can build some things

Here and now

Which will last for a time

Marble outlasts wood

The blues is the aquifer that nourishes

All our music, so long as there are people

There will be blues; and martyrdom

Will be remembered longer

Than any exaggerated homespun yarn

So build. Build places and institutions

Make music and reputation

Build houses plant gardens and settle down

But know that change is permanent

Structures will crumble organizations will implode

Memories and communion are indestructible

And this is where freedom is and know if you

Remember and work

Work and remember

Freedom once restored by refining fire

Will reappear just when

It seems that it is lost

It's only a month and a half

From March 6

To April 21."

The elevator called as the lobby filled and the day began

They left me and faded to a succession of E7 A7 and B7 chords

Instead of pushing the close button on the panel

I held the door and shared the space

III

Fear living dead

The zombie-fog psyche, the contagion spread into our spaces

A thousand mechanical circuit-breaking cancellations

Proved by statistics:

Graduations art festivals funerals beaches parks gyms
unconcealed smiles handshakes back patting playoffs
pageants removal of braces proms glad handing drivers tests
classrooms haircuts embraces

And day and night lost the will of action

April, indeed, is cruel

So we follow silent rules into the death of spring

Nobody laughs

A moratorium on new memories

And full recognition of faces

Nothing to eat nowhere to sit down

No Texas Outdoor Musical in Palo Duro Canyon

No East Texas Shakespeare Festival

No South by Southwest

No Houston Livestock Show and Rodeo

No church

The dire poison washed over as we let

The pause

Penetrate and strangle our plans

We had intended to go to the Museum of Modern Art, 5th floor

The genius epileptic's starry night vision called

But barbed wire barricaded the door

And a sun-bleached cow skull

Warned us and cut off our access

Left instead with The Persistence of Memory

As in a dream where we walked without end

Opened and forgotten impressions

Real and imagined slowly rose

I whispered to myself: time memory and future

Are all being stripped away but yet they remain

Still in perpetual readiness

In our waiting we remember:

The Library of Alexandria

Virgil tossing the Aeneid into flames

Cotton's Beowulf scorching fire

Emily Dickinson directing her estate to burn her papers

The Texas Capitol 1881

Brooklyn Theater 1876

Bastrop 2011

911 attacks

Notre Dame de Paris 2019

Memories conjured present fears

And this future hard conjecture:

Fire on the 5th floor of MOMA

What then?

Ten thousand broom swishes

Sweeping dust broken glass and charred remains

Clearing rot and disinfecting

A hundred thousand life-giving brush strokes

Mosaics assembled tapestries woven shards collected

Fragments shored

We have been home

The comfort of silence and waiting

And in our waiting we have faith

That out of the quiet comes culture and

Out of culture life

In the blistering Texas heat

Colors steadily emerge and dance

Scenes familiar and unfamiliar materialized

Patterns and faces realized

Older memories renewed and transplanted

Newer memories now begun

Andy Marilyn Vincent Pablo Henri Salvador

Not a Texan among you

Dragged unsuspecting East to West

From comfortable Manhattan sophistication

To roost here of all places

We've always had a belligerent streak

Davy Crockett spoke about us for us and with us

When he said with no magnanimity in defeat:

You may all go to hell and I will go to Texas

He did and lasted a month

Like archetypal Texas bringers and builders that followed
him

James Huckins and William Tryon

Swante Palm

Velma and Kay Kimbell

Bill Mead

Dr. A.J. Armstrong

Not ones to wilt in heat nor shrink in adversity

They pushed acted cultivated toiled

We grafted you into our space

Now let's be human together:

Our lives

Comedy beauty awfulness hardness

Tragedy victory hardship comfort

Ultimately are the same

Texas *tejas* friendship

Do your work alongside us

Continually at rest always faring forward

With deeper engagement

Enduring relationships continual renewal

Living dead and yet to be

Recalled imagined and loved

In that Midtown Manhattan museum

And this museum in this field

In harmonious movement remembering anticipating

Quick now here now always

Raise your head

Be free

And catch a squinting glimpse of what was there

and is now here

and will endure

for a season

because it is loved:

Beyond the ice-clad Panhandle barbed wire border

  See whispering shimmering wheat farms bleeding
Kansas Nebraska railroad headquarters Badlands buffalo
herds nomadic Sioux warriors whiplashed oil wells fortunes
won and lost

Into the Piney Woods at dusk half-light

  See Caddo farmers harvesting pumpkins sunflowers
corn wild French traders beaver raccoon pelts Spindletop

Over beaches into the Gulf of Mexico from a rooftop at
sunrise

See salty wild oyster harvests cruise ships returning
rattling greasy breakfast plates humming oil platforms
Fredericksburg founders disembarking swindled landless the
long march north begins

And if you rumble down a sun-punished

Dust-lashed caliche road

Bordered by weed-choked ditches

And pull your truck in here you would find

This place

Our beginning again

Culture sewn with sweat labor

Gathering past present future now

IV

The dove returning brings a sign

Half-light colors begin to burn

The waters then start to drain

The dove next time did not return

Stones here stacked in dry design

Hard ground now dry but for tears

Thistle and dust once cursed now kissed

But still we choose flood or flood

Death or redeemed from drowning by baptism in blood

Water is life

Water is death

Consider Phlebas

Who devised this awkward scheme? Love.

Love is the One

Whose hand stretched the bow

Across the big burnt-orange sky

Which we can no more coerce

Than we can summon bluebonnets

Or cajole a hurricane

Consider Galveston 1900

Consider Harvey

But also consider

Houston rising up out of the waters

Just as Pastor Burleson lifted the General

Millions of hands lifted our City

His sins flowed down Little Rocky Creek

And into The Brazos

And our City raised its head and stood

Gave thanks

And became someone

Someone once again free

V

It is told by our Storytellers

That before the age of barbed wire

A steer driven from deep down in Texas as far as Kansas

Would sometimes turn around

Walk back along the trail and eventually

Arrive where he started

Words and writing

Simplicity and the dance

Place and soil and failing sunset light

The persistence of return

To a simple place of white limestone

Wind and hand-hewn red oak beam

Simple worship through words

Remembrance and gratitude

Rising and falling

Simple costly complete

Slow contemplations containing beginning and end

All that has gone before and all that will be is here

Now

History is

Now and Texas

Tomorrow with reliance on who we

Know ourselves to be

And who we yet hope and imagine and strive to be

We act and build and work and sweat

Study and narrate cultivate nourish fight and sing

We will not stop and as we build

We will see once again and know again

That the timeless moments of time Texas past are here

Forever and always

May our children and our grandchildren belong more than us

Beyond that we can hope

For our great great grandparents and great grandchildren

Together in friendship

In the harvest around the pit on the field

Around the cradle

In the pew

At the table

In the poetry and the song

On the hunt in the oil patch

In our cities and our towns

Juntos en Amistad

Next year's wheat fields dancing in the wind

Bluebonnets silently serenading the shifting sunset mosaic

And cousins gathering in a dappled-light pecan grove

Lacking precision and coercion

But overflowing with beauty

Felt and known but not corralled

Like your dream that dissipates once described

As if you could saddle a sunset

Or summarize a handshake

Or grab hickory smoke with a catcher's mitt

This we can savor and tell and embrace and build

Preserve the solitary star

Now lift your head and stand

Be free

Your children will bless your name

My wife, Shona Cole, painting of a copy of Van Gogh's Starry Night at The Grounds 1488

Beyond State Line Road, 1992

Oil painting by Shona Cole

Cadillac Ranch

By Madeleine Frost

Be Someone is a reoccurring piece of graffiti above Interstate 45 in Houston, Texas.

By Shona Cole

Made in the USA
Coppell, TX
05 May 2021

54986385R00079